WE LOVE PIZZA
Everything you want to know about your number one food

by Elenia Beretta

This book was edited and designed
by Little Gestalten.

Edited by Robert Klanten and Maria-Elisabeth Niebius

Texts by David Henry Wilson and Elenia Beretta

Design and layout by Melanie Ullrich
Typeface: Proxima Nova by Mark Simonson

Printed by Grafisches Centrum Cuno GmbH & Co. KG, Calbe (Saale)
Made in Germany

Published by Little Gestalten, Berlin 2021
ISBN 978-3-96704-705-9

For more information, and to order books,
please visit www.little.gestalten.com.

Bibliographic information published by the Deutsche Nationalbibliothek.
The Deutsche Nationalbibliothek lists this publication in the Deutsche
Nationalbibliografie; detailed bibliographic data are available online at
www.dnb.de.

This book was printed on
paper certified according
to the standards of the FSC®.

WE LOVE PIZZA

Everything you want to know about
your number one food

Elenia Beretta

LITTLE
GESTALTEN

THE WORLD'S FAVORITE FOOD

The world is full of people,
And people have to eat,
And if they had to choose a dish,
There's one that's hard to beat.

You make it and you bake it,
Or you buy it in a shop.
It can be soft or crunchy,
And have lots of things on top.

It's simple but delicious—
That's how it's earned its fame.
Have you now guessed what it is?
Yes, PIZZA is its name!

PICK A PIECE OF PIZZA

Pizzas can be round or square,
In different shapes and sizes,
And sometimes what is in or on them
Is full of big surprises.

PIZZA AL METRO comes from Sorrento in Italy. "Metro" means "meter" (39 inches)—not the subway!—and that's how long it is. If you want to eat it all in one go, it would help if you were a crocodile.

DETROIT STYLE PIZZA is made with a special cheese called Wisconsin brick cheese. If you can't eat it, you can build a house with it. (Just kidding! It's sold in brick-shaped packets.)

CALZONE is the folded one. "Calzone" means "trousers," but you won't find any legs inside it.

FLAMMKUCHEN ("flame cake")
comes from Alsace, a region
between France and Germany. It looks
as if it's got freckles, but those
spots are just yummy bits of bacon.

LAHMACUN comes from Turkey and
Armenia. It's all rolled up like a sleeping
hedgehog, with minced meat on top
and some super spicy vegetables inside,
like onions, peppers, and garlic.

CHICAGO DEEP DISH looks
more like a bowl than a pizza,
but that's just an excuse to
put more and more cheese
and tomato sauce in it.

Everything in New York is big—
especially the NEW YORK PIZZA.
You'll need to fold it
before you can hold it.

HOW MANY?

How many pizzas do people munch?
Here are some numbers for you to crunch.

Who would have thought that
Germans consume more
pizza than the average Italian?
One hundred slices a year.

Americans eat about 350 slices
of pizza per second, which
means every person eats about
46 slices a year.

Italians are surprisingly not on
the winner's podium. It might
be too difficult to decide ... pizza
or pasta, pasta or pizza?

The World Champions!
An average Norwegian
eats 11 pizzas per year.
They love the frozen ones!

In Brazil, they're nuts about
pizzas. They eat one million
of them a day.

Pizzas brighten up all weathers.
No wonder British people eat
4.5 kg (10 lb.) of them every year.

WHEN WAS THE
FIRST PIZZA BORN?

It must have been thousands of years ago,
But here are the only facts we know.

The kind of pizza we all know and love was born in Naples, in southern Italy. It's the third-biggest city in Italy, after Rome and Milan, and is at least 2,500 years old. But the oldest known pizza sellers only go back as far as 1738.

In those days, pizzas were sold on the streets and were mainly regarded as a simple food for the poor. It wasn't until 1830 that the first known pizzeria opened its doors in Naples as a proper restaurant. It was called Antica Pizzeria Port'Alba. It changed the whole image of pizza, and you'll be amazed to hear that it's still there today, baking all kinds of pizzas for all kinds of people.

QUEEN MARGHERITA

To what does this Queen owe her fame?
To a special pizza that bears her name!

In 1889, King Umberto and Queen Margherita were visiting Naples. Kings and queens are special people, and of course they wanted special food: a pizza nobody else had ever tasted. And so the chef Raffaele Esposito had a problem: what if he cooked a new pizza and they didn't like it? He could be in big trouble. So can you guess what he did?

PIZZA FOR A QUEEN

Raffaele Esposito cooked several pizzas, and the one that Queen Margherita liked best was green, white, and red—the colors of the Italian flag!

THE RED
is tomato sauce.

THE WHITE
is mozzarella
cheese.

THE GREEN
is basil.

THE DOUGH
is made with
flour, water, yeast,
and salt.

THE CRUST
is soft and
elastic—easy to fold.

Margherita, Margherita,
Everyone heats her and eats her.
Instead of being a powerful queen,
She's now a much-loved pizza.

The diameter
is a maximum
of 35 cm (14 in.).

The crunchy
crust is 1 to 2 cm
(0.4 to 0.8 in.) thick.

The thickness of
the central part
is approximately
0.25 cm (0.1 in.).

The chef has only 10 seconds
to put on the toppings. Pizza
Margherita is baked in a wood
oven at a temperature of up
to 485°C (905°F).

It takes just 60 to 90 seconds
to cook! The pizza is served
piping hot. It is best to eat it
straight from the oven.

HOW TO MAKE A PIZZA

Before we eat it, we bake it.
And before we bake it, we make it!

Chef Charlotte from Naples
will show us how to make a
pizza with our hands, a spoon,
and a bowl.

WE NEED 1 KG (2.2 LB.) OF FLOUR.
There are lots of different sorts,
and the one we shall use is "pizza
flour," or type 00, which is soft
wheat flour, white and starchy.

BREWER'S YEAST.
Just 7 g (0.25 oz.) of
dry yeast will make
the dough swell a
lot before it's baked.

SEA SALT.
If you can't pop down to the
beach and evaporate some
fresh sea water, then do
what Charlotte did: she bought
some at the supermarket.

A CAN OF WHOLE
TOMATOES
(400 g [14 oz]),
1 onion, 1 tablespoon
of BASIL, and some
SALT and PEPPER.

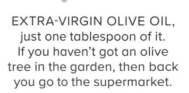

THEN WE NEED WATER.
The weight of the water should
be 80% of the weight of the
flour, so for 1 kg (2.2 lb.) of flour,
we'll use 800 ml (27 fl. oz.)
of lukewarm water.

EXTRA-VIRGIN OLIVE OIL,
just one tablespoon of it.
If you haven't got an olive
tree in the garden, then back
you go to the supermarket.

MOZZARELLA CHEESE
(or any other type you prefer)
and BASIL that you put
fresh on the pizza once
it comes out of the oven.

That's what you need. Have you read it through?
OK, for two pizzas, here's what you do.

1 Add the yeast to the flour and mix.

2 Pour in the water and mix. Wait for 5 minutes. (Sing a song.)

3 Add the salt and oil, and mix it all for about 10 minutes.

 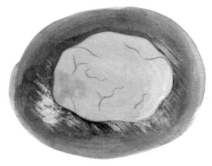 

4 Let it rest for 15 minutes, covered by a cloth. You can rest too—but no need to cover yourself with a cloth.

5 Put some flour on the pastry board and put the dough on it.

6 With the help of something flat, fold the dough from right to center, and rest for 10 minutes.

7 Fold from left to center, and rest for 10 minutes.

8 Top to center, rest for 10 minutes.

9 Bottom to center, rest for 10 minutes.

10 Phew, this is exhausting... Stop folding and resting! Take a deep breath, and make the dough into a ball, but don't kick or throw it!

11 Grease a bowl with oil, put the dough in, cover it with plastic wrap, and put it at the bottom of the fridge in the vegetable box (because it's not so cold there).

12 Now the dough needs a break. This is why: yeast needs time to make the dough huge and fluffy. If you used the dough right away, it would grow bigger and bigger in your tummy, and that would hurt.

TWO HOURS
close to a warm heater is the minimum for the yeast to start its work.

FOUR HOURS
is very good when you want a pizza for tonight's dinner.

22 HOURS
makes Charlotte's perfect restaurant-quality pizza dough.

13 The dough should have doubled in size.

14 Take the ball out of the bowl and separate it into two smaller balls.

15 Take one ball and put it on the baking tray, tapping it lightly with your fingertips to spread it out.

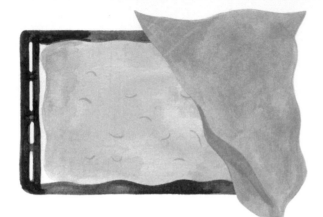

16 While you prepare the tomato sauce, cover the dough with a cloth so that it can rest again. Turn on the oven (250°C [482°F] or the maximum).

17 Chop up the onion and fry it quickly, add the tomatoes, cover the pan, and cook for 5 minutes. Add salt and 1 tablespoon of chopped basil, and turn off the heat. If it's too liquid, take the lid off the pan for a minute or two.

18 Use a spoon to spread a layer of sauce over the dough.

IT'S BAKING TIME!

Put the dough on the lower shelf,
Making sure you don't burn yourself.
Bake for 10 minutes, then add the cheese,
Plus whatever toppings you please.
Use the middle shelf for the final heat,
And in 10 minutes add the basil and eat!

SNEAK A PEEK INTO A PIZZERIA

A STONE SCRUBBER removes burned cheese crusts from the oven.

WOODEN PIZZA PEELS slide the pizza into the oven and help you to get it out without burning your hands.

THE OVEN BRUSH reaches far back into the oven to get all the dust and dirt out.

The pizzeria has a special wood-burning oven, which has a dome and is twice as hot as your oven at home. With the dough already prepared, Charlotte puts on the toppings, lays the pizza on a long shovel (it has to be long, because otherwise the chef would cook herself as well as the pizza), and into the oven it goes. A couple of minutes later, out it comes, shining like gold. And the waiter comes racing to your table, because nobody wants cold pizza.

HOW TO EAT A PIZZA

Equipment to be supplied by you:
A mouth with teeth, and a hand (or two).
There is no how-to-eat-pizza law,
But try not to drop it on the floor.

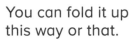

You can fold it up
this way or that.

You can cut it from the
middle to the crust, or from
the crust to the middle.

You can pour olive oil
into the center and
dip the crust into it.

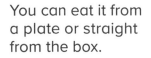

You can eat it from a plate or straight from the box.

You can eat it with your hands, or use a knife and fork.

Do you know Pacman, the greatest computer game hero of all time? The Japanese video game designer Toru Iwatani came up with his design while looking at his pizza, minus one slice!

PIZZA RECORDS

One day you'll be a great pizza maker,
But will you be a record breaker?

Scott Wiener from New York City has the largest collection of pizza boxes in the world. He has over 1,500 boxes.

A group of pizza chefs from Rome created the biggest pizza ever baked. It covered a total surface area of 1,261 m² (13,580 ft²). This is approximately 15,000 times the size of a regular pizza!

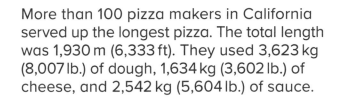

More than 100 pizza makers in California served up the longest pizza. The total length was 1,930 m (6,333 ft). They used 3,623 kg (8,007 lb.) of dough, 1,634 kg (3,602 lb.) of cheese, and 2,542 kg (5,604 lb.) of sauce.

Brian Dwyer from Philadelphia has the largest collection of pizza-related items in the world. He has over 560 different objects, including stickers, comic books, and the cover of an LP by the group Fat Boys. The collection is open to the public.

THE PIZZA CONQUERS AMERICA

*How did pizzas make their way
From Italy to the USA?*

In the late 19th century, a lot of Italian immigrants arrived in the USA. At first, they were the only people who wanted to eat their pizzas, but now Americans eat a billion pizzas a year.

PIZZERIAS

Once it was food for poorer residents,
But now it's eaten by princes and presidents.

In the old days, pizzas were sold by street vendors, mainly to poor people, but when the first pizzerias in the USA were opened, more and more toppings were introduced, and more and more people became pizza fans. Roberta's Pizzeria was once a garage, Lucali's Pizzeria was a laundry service, and Buddy's used to be a sports bar.

PIZZAS FROM AROUND THE WORLD

*There are different tastes east, west, north, south,
But there's a topping for every mouth!*

CAPRICCIOSA

"Capriccio" is Italian for
"whim." And "whim"
means whatever you like.
It's a pizza potpourri and
usually comes with artichoke,
mushrooms, and ham.

HAWAIIAN PIZZA

was invented by a Mr. Panopoulos
in 1962, using ham and pineapple.
He lived in Canada, so why Hawaiian?
Because that's where the pineapple
came from. People said he couldn't mix
sour and sweet. People were wrong!
It's one of the most popular
pizzas in the world.

This one is special because the chefs use ingredients that are grown in one particular American state. Can you guess which one? Here's a clue: it begins with "C" and rhymes with "didn't I warn ya?" Yeah! This one is called CALIFORNIA.

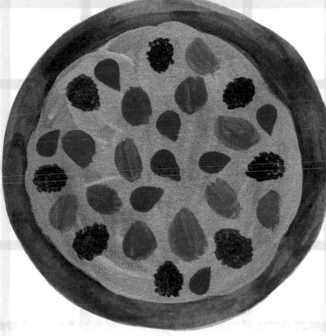

24K

is a luxury pizza covered with edible 24-karat gold that costs 2,000 dollars. The gold gives the pizza a shiny wow effect but adds no flavor. Don't you prefer the liquid gold called olive oil?

BOX PIZZA

The owner of a pizzeria in Brooklyn noticed that some customers ordered their pizza in a box, then ate it in the restaurant and threw the box away. So he made a box that is a pizza in itself.

MARINARA

is the oldest Italian pizza, created in 1734. It was the sailors' favorite, the "marinaio." Garlic, oregano, and olive oil: simply the best—even without cheese!

QUATTRO FORMAGGI
(4 cheeses pizza)

Mozzarella, Gorgonzola, and whatever cheeses they make in your region. How many cheeses can you name?

The PIZZA-KEBAB

is a mixture of Turkish chicken, lamb, or beef, and Italian cheese and sauce, and it was invented in Sweden. Rumor has it that the Turks and Italians don't like it, but the Swedes love it!

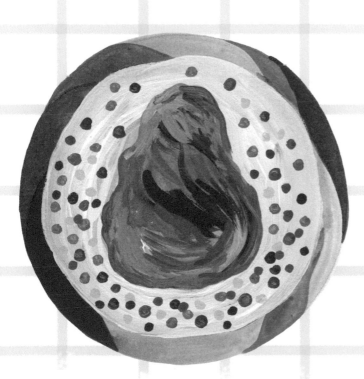

OKONOMIYAKI

is a Japanese pizza (the name
means "cook what you like")
made with flour, yam, and shredded
cabbage, and toppings like
pork, octopus, and squid.

RAINBOW PIZZA

Multicolored icing, sprinkles,
Pop Rocks, cotton candy...
If you have a sweet tooth,
this is for you.

COAT OF ARMS PIZZA

The toppings are kangaroo and emu, and you'll only find these on the coat of arms of the country that is the smallest continent in the world—Australia.

PIZZA CRUNCH

A mini calzone fried in oil is a favorite in Scotland. To make the dish even more crunchy, it is served with chips. It is also served as street food in Naples.

There's a legend in China that pizza is an adaptation of the SCALLION PANCAKE, brought back to Italy by Marco Polo. (Scallions are a sort of spring onion.) Please don't tell the Italians.

CACIO E PEPE

means "cheese and pepper."
It is a worldwide pasta dish
turned into a pizza. Ice cubes
are added to keep the top
moist and the bottom crisp.
Sounds cool!

KHACHAPURI

is from Georgia. It is believed to
be the only pizza in the world
that looks at you with its eggy
eye before you eat it.

PIZZERIA PEOPLE

*The people you see standing here
Are somehow linked to our pizzeria.*

CHARLOTTE
is the chef who
brilliantly bakes the
perfect pizzas.

WALTER
is the waiter who's
willing and able
to bring the pizza
to your table.

FIONA
is the owner of the
pizzeria, and she
hopes you'll come
again. And again
and again.

DAVID
delivers the piping
hot pizzas to the
homes of hungry
customers.

GRETA,
the greengrocer
who sells the
vegetables to
the pizzeria.

BORIS
is the butcher
who sells the
meat that
people eat as
a special treat.

WOODY
cuts trees into logs
and brings the logs to
heat the oven for
Charlotte to cook the
pizza, for Walter to
bring to your table, for
you to eat and enjoy
so much that you
will come back again
and again to
Fiona's pizzeria.

FERDINAND
is the farmer
who grows the
vegetables that
he sells to ...

CHERYL
makes the cheeses,
and if you like
cheese, then please
choose Cheryl's
champion cheeses.

NOTHING CAN STOP A GOOD PIZZA

It doesn't matter where you live,
Or where you work and play,
Order the pizza that you want,
And soon it's on its way.

In Alaska there are places you can't get to on foot, or with a bike or car. And so your pizza has to be delivered by plane! Until a couple of years ago, the airport pizzeria in the city of Nome, Alaska, sent pizzas by plane to all the nearby villages. But they had to order at least 30 pizzas (at 10 dollars each).

In towns and cities, delivery is often done by bike or motorcycle, as they can get through the traffic more easily. And as you know, pizza tastes best when eaten soon after baking.

If you'd like to keep a stock
Of pizzas you've chosen,
It's as easy as pie:
You can get pizzas frozen.

Frozen pizzas were invented in America in the 1950s, and as refrigerators and freezers became more and more common, frozen pizzas became more and more popular. You don't have to go to Alaska. You'll find them in any supermarket.

THE PIZZA BOX
was invented in the mid-1960s to make home delivery and takeaway super simple.

It's made of cardboard and keeps your pizza hot.

OUT OF THIS WORLD

One order came from the strangest place:
The customer was in outer space!

In 2001, an American pizza restaurant chain delivered a 15 cm (6 in.) salami pizza by rocket to Russian cosmonaut Yury Usachov at the International Space Station. You cannot send a regular pizza into space. It took one year to invent a version that could make this long journey. And it cost 1 million dollars. An astronomical price for an astronomical pizza.

PIZZA: THE FINEST FOOD
FOR FAMILY AND FRIENDS

All of us love pizza.
There's a smile on every face.
If the world was one big pizza,
It would be a happy place.